What We Wear

Dressing Up Around the World

Maya Ajmera ● **Elise Hofer Derstine** ● **Cynthia Pon**

A GLOBAL FUND FOR
Children
BOOK

Charlesbridge

Uzbekistan

Finland

Israel

Mali

Bangladesh

South Africa

Chile

Around the world, we dress up to have fun!

India

Turkey

We dance and play . . .

USA

Switzerland

... wearing feathers, beads, and flowers.

Papua New Guinea

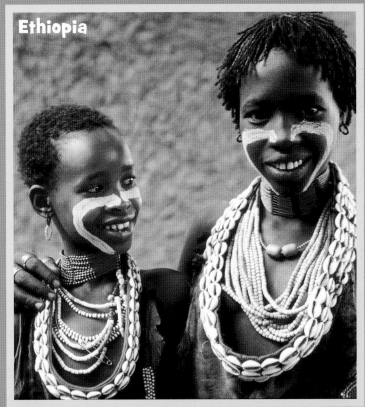

Ethiopia

Dressing up means celebrating who we are . . .

Peru

Japan

United Kingdom

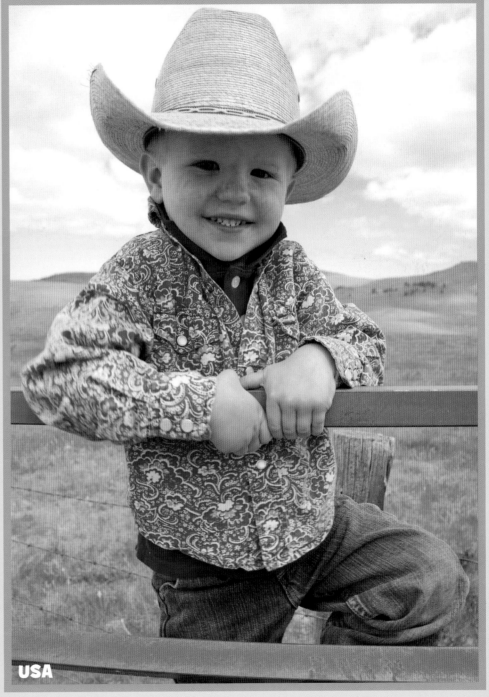

USA

... and what we believe.

Australia

Nepal

Canada

Indonesia

United Kingdom

We wear special clothes to go to school . . .

India

Uganda

Japan

... play games, and be part of a team.

USA

United Kingdom

Malawi

We wear all the colors of the rainbow . . .

Ecuador

Ukraine

Iran

Brazil

Martinique

Canada

... paint our faces, and wear masks.

Panama

Dressing up means playing pretend!

Singapore

USA

Kazakhstan

Sweden

Belize

We wear what we like and feel our best.

India

Niger

Egypt

Canada

USA

Belize

Guatemala

Martinique

Panama

Ecuador

Brazil

Peru

Chile

The children in this book come from all over the world.

DISCOVER DIFFERENT CULTURES

Visit a Folk Festival

A folk festival is a celebration where people get together to share culture through music, food, crafts, and dance. Children and their families who participate dress up in traditional clothing, often wearing styles that were popular many years ago. Find out if folk festivals happen where you live or somewhere nearby. If your town has a tourism office, they will be able to help you. It doesn't matter what culture is being celebrated—no matter what, you'll see exciting things and learn something new!

Kenya

Germany

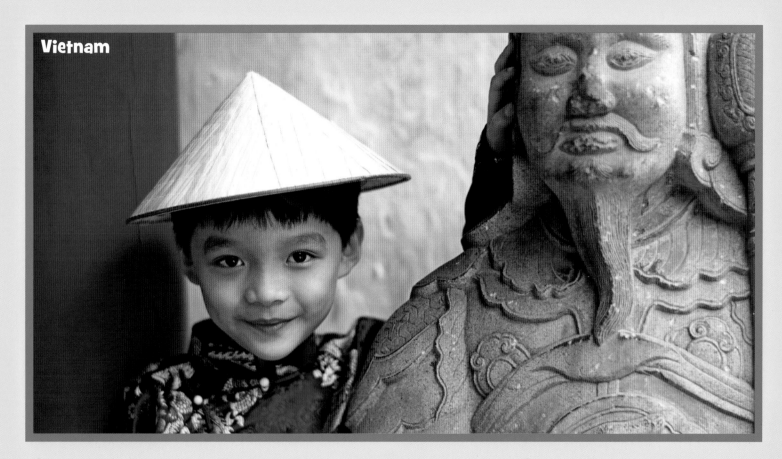

Vietnam

Check Out a Museum

Museums are great places to look at clothing. History museums may have gowns from past centuries, uniforms worn by soldiers, or clothing worn by indigenous peoples. Anthropology museums may feature hand-woven shawls, clothing made from animal skins, and beaded jewelry. Cultural museums and folk-art museums are also good places to look for fun and unusual dress styles.

Ask About Clothes of the Past

Ask to see pictures of your parents or grandparents from when they were children. What are they wearing in the photographs? How are the clothes different from yours? Styles of dress change over time, and you might find out that your grandmother wore only skirts, or your dad liked to wear cowboy boots. They might even have some old clothing packed away that you could try on—an old-fashioned hat, a hand-woven vest, or a wedding dress.

LEARN ABOUT YOUR HERITAGE

Find Connections Around the World

Maybe your family or a friend's family came to your country from another part of the world, either recently or a long time ago. How did people dress when they lived there? You might discover they dressed just like you, or very differently. Can you come up with some reasons for the differences?

Ghana

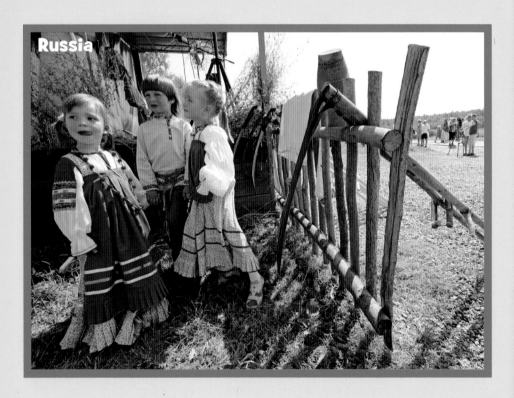

Russia

LET'S PRETEND!

Make a Mask

Children all over the world wear masks for festivals, holidays, religious ceremonies, and just for fun. Masks are easy to make using cardboard, recycled paper, or a paper plate for the face. You can decorate your mask with paint, dried flowers, paper cutouts, or fallen leaves. Ask an adult to help you cut eyeholes big enough for you to see through. Be creative: you're sure to have a mask that is one-of-a-kind.

Discover Costumes Wherever You Look

Costumes don't have to be fancy or complicated. Make a crown out of paper and wear a long piece of fabric as a robe, and you can become a king or queen in a few minutes! Tie flower stems together to make a long necklace. Paint your face with whiskers and a black nose, and you can be a cat. There is no limit to what you can do if you use your imagination.

Sri Lanka

USA

The authors wish to thank Victoria Dunning and Laurel Fiorelli for their contributions to the development of this book.

Photo Credits

Thailand

For my naniji, who always dressed with style and elegance—M. A.

For my mother, the most stylish woman in the room,
and for my father, who knows it—E. H. D.

For colors that grow, for hands that sew and knit,
and for all those who have wrapped me in love—C. P.

What We Wear was developed by The Global Fund for Children (www.globalfundforchildren.org),
a nonprofit organization committed to advancing the dignity of children and youth around the
world. Global Fund for Children books teach young people to value diversity and help them become
productive and caring citizens of the world.

Afghanistan

Developed by The Global Fund for Children
1101 Fourteenth Street NW, Suite 420
Washington, DC 20005
(202) 331-9003
www.globalfundforchildren.org

Published by Charlesbridge
85 Main Street
Watertown, MA 02472
(617) 926-0329
www.charlesbridge.com

Part of the proceeds from this book's sales will be donated to The Global
Fund for Children to support innovative community-based organizations
that serve the world's most vulnerable children and youth. Details about
the donation of royalties can be obtained by writing to Charlesbridge
Publishing and The Global Fund for Children.

Library of Congress Cataloging-in-Publication Data
Ajmera, Maya.
    What we wear : dressing up around the world / Maya Ajmera,
Elise Hofer Derstine, Cynthia Pon.
        p. cm.
    ISBN 978-1-58089-416-6 (reinforced for library use)
    ISBN 978-1-58089-417-3 (softcover)
1. Clothing and dress--Juvenile literature. I. Hofer Derstine, Elise.
II. Pon, Cynthia. III. Title.
GT518.A56 2012
391--dc22   2011014319

Printed in Korea
(hc) 10 9 8 7 6 5 4 3 2
(sc) 10 9 8 7 6 5

Display type and text type set in Grilled Cheese
Color separations by KHL Chroma Graphics, Singapore
Printed by Sung In Printing in Gunpo-Si, Kyonggi-Do, Korea
Production supervision by Brian G. Walker
Designed by Susan Mallory Sherman